JOURNEYS

Words of Wisdom

Other books in the
Words of Wisdom series

The Dalai Lama
Nelson Mandela
Pope John Paul II

JOURNEYS

Timeless Travel Quotations

Words of Wisdom

Selected quotes compiled by

MARGARET GEE

MACMILLAN
Pan Macmillan Australia

For my twin sister Christine Gee, who has inspired so many
people to journey to wild and remote places

First published 2000 in Macmillan by Pan Macmillan Australia Pty Limited
St Martins Tower, 31 Market Street, Sydney

National Library of Australia
Cataloguing-in-Publication data:

Journeys: timeless travel quotations – words of wisdom.

ISBN 0 7329 1056 0.

1. Travel – Quotations, Maxims, etc. 2. Travelers – Quotations.
I. Gee, Margaret.

082

Typeset by Post Pre-Press
Printed by Tien Wah Press, Singapore

Acknowledgments

Many thanks to the dedicated publishing team at Pan Macmillan. My sincere appreciation for assistance in the research to John Borthwick, PhD, and Tricia Carroll.

A donation from sales of this book will be made to Sir Edmund Hillary's Himalayan Trust and Amnesty International.

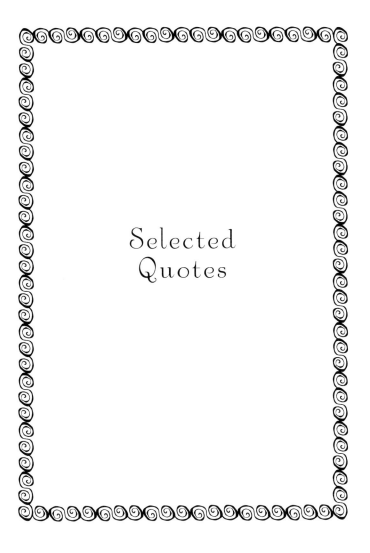

Selected
Quotes

Travel gently, stay cool. Try to leave no sign of
your presence except agreeable memories and
when it all goes wrong, remember, you chose to
go there, so make the best of it.

Sir Christian Bonington, CBE – mountaineer and author

Imagine lying on your back in a truck driving along railroad tracks with a bowling ball on your chest. Lift-off in the Space Shuttle feels like that. During the first stage, when the two solid rocket boosters and three main engines are accelerating the Shuttle with seven million pounds of thrust, the ride is quite bumpy.

The single most incredible moment of the flight occurs at MECO (main engine cut-off) when the 3-G rocket ride ends and the Og orbit begins, all in one heartbeat. Suddenly, everything is floating, your pencil, parachute straps, your arms and legs. Unstrapping from your seat, you float around the cabin to explore a magical new world. This is space flight!

Kathryn C. Thornton – US astronaut

My travels help me cheat death by making life longer and richer: I leave home for a week, a fortnight, a month and I return a month, a year, a lifetime later, with a heart account full of memories that no-one can ever steal.

Brigitte Muir – first Australian woman to summit Mt Everest, author, from *The Wind in My Hair*

It is one of the Great Truths of Travel that as a single female traveller, you'll be spotted by the sleaziest bloke in the hotel bar and he'll pay the pianist to tinkle 'Strangers in the Night' and get the barman to mix you a 'Liquid Orgasm' with his compliments. If a single male traveller, it's a GTT that the sexy Filipina torch singer in the hotel will be married to the barman who was possibly separated at birth from his identical twin, Godzilla. It is a GTT that you will not discover this fact until you've asked the barman to mix her a Liquid Orgasm with your compliments.

Susan Kurosawa – travel editor for the *Australian*, from *The Joy of Travel*, and author of *Coasting: A Year by the Bay*

Travelling in Tibet is not only about spectacular scenery and adventurous expeditions, it can be a spiritual journey or the fulfilment of a long awaited dream. Over the years my travels into the remote and rural parts of this land have made me realise that the lifestyle of the local Tibetans has not changed, along with their sacred Buddhist values, and undying hope of a 'free Tibet' and the return of His Holiness the fourteenth Dalai Lama.

Tashi Yangzom – Thor Travel, Adelaide

A selective memory is the greatest asset of any traveller or adventurer. When the mist comes in and you can't find the path, you tell yourself, as you have done so often before, that you will never return to these wretched slopes, jungles, streets again. And when you do return home, this deft attribute blots out the hardship and the fear and you begin to plan again to go where you have not travelled before.

Peter Hillary – Hillary Adventures International,
New Zealand

Through travel, make an impact and change people's lives; expose them to the excitement and natural wonders and cultures of the world and show them there is a lot more to life than business, money, hedonism and social steeple-jacking.

Geoffrey Kent – chairman and chief executive officer, Abercrombie & Kent

Even after viewing the vast Himalayan ranges
your most memorable experiences are those
shared with the local villagers you meet on the
remote mountain trail.

Garry Weare – author, from *Trekking the Indian Himalaya*

On my first trip to Nepal, the customs officer at Kathmandu airport was sitting cross-legged on top of his desk, stamping passports in a dreamy but deliberate fashion. And I thought: Yeah, this place is different. On my first trip to Antarctica I was so excited when I stepped out of the warm fug of the plane onto the ice that I gulped a big breath of crisp polar air so cold that the alveoli inside my lungs felt as if they had been sprayed with liquid nitrogen. Travel, to me, are those blinding instants in time when your whole conception of the way the world should work is forever altered. When your body and soul are so alert that the passage of time is altered. And you can never quite be the same again.

Greg Mortimer – mountaineer and co-founder of Aurora Expeditions

The plane climbs above the Borneo jungle which for the last weeks has sheltered, exhausted and enthralled us. Somewhere below are giant lace-winged butterflies, an infinite variety of known and unknown species, and some of the earth's last rainforest people.

At last we can see the extent of the logging. As far as the horizon, the forest is gridded by the brown scars of timber roads. Eroded soil pours from them into the rivers. In twenty years, 2.8 million hectares, or 30 per cent of Sarawak's forests were felled. Much more has been licensed for future logging. If the jungle below were a precious object, say a Vermeer painting, the gouges raked across it would be reviled as a crime against culture. If it were an animal, these scars would be something beyond sadism. Instead, it is the 15 million-year-old lungs of our planet, the Garden of Eden of earth's gene pool. Yet beyond the cry of the reclusive, illiterate Penans, the systematic excision of its parts hardly raises an eyebrow.

John Borthwick, PhD – travel writer, photographer and author, from *The Circumference of the Knowable World*

If I truly wanted to journey into the passion for cars, I'd need, literally, to drive into it.

By its very nature, the journey would have to be a physical one, a road trip intimately bound up with the road itself.

It seemed a pleasingly elegant idea. Yet even as I planned a rough route, leaving plenty of room for serendipity, I was uncomfortably aware that journeys have a way of creating their own momentum. They take you places and reveal things you never knew you were looking for. Once I put myself on the road, I'd lay myself open to the way experience toys with fine ideas and tosses them into chaos, forcing you deeper and further than you ever wanted. I wasn't sure if I was ready for this.

Lesley Hazleton – author, from *Driving to Detroit*

Apart from crocodiles there are no person-eating wild beasts in the Australian bush, although snakes and spiders have despatched the odd unlucky traveller. These instances are so rare they can be discounted. If there are any instances of death by belligerent kangaroos or emus I am unaware of them. The only fear I have when selecting a bush camp in the late afternoon is some other traveller will see me and come up and camp nearby for 'security'. Security against what for God's sake?

Tim Bowden – author, from *Penelope Goes West: On the Road from Sydney to Margaret River and Back*

My personal dream for many years was to share the summit of the Sydney Harbour Bridge with everyone. I will never forget my first climb. My heart skipped a beat, and then another, in climbing the King Post Ladder to go on to the arch. On reaching the top it is: 'Wow! Wow!' The greatest reward is to watch the exhilaration on the faces of climbers as they conquer their own personal Olympics.

Paul B. Cave – chairman of Bridgeclimb Sydney

Being the first person in history to have walked
to both the South Pole and the North Pole is not a
journey I would recommend for most, but it
enabled me to experience first-hand my passion
for polar history. Also, at minus 51°C decisions
become critical and in a sense it's a journey you
never fully return from. You also never want to
walk anywhere again! The unexpected revelations
of those journeys was to discover the devastating
effects of the hole in the ozone layer and the
havoc polar pollution is having on our planet.
That is why I now spend my life giving lectures
inviting companies to get involved in projects
which clean up the mess we have left behind. If
that can be achieved future generations will be
able to enjoy what we travellers now take for
granted.

Robert Swan, OBE – British polar explorer

There comes a moment in the life of every traveller when a terrible realisation strikes: there are only so many journeys left. The youthful notion that a lifetime is more than enough to see a whole world is replaced by the sense that your income and your holiday entitlements are going to keep you at home or at work for most of every year. And that could mean you're looking forward to only twenty more voyages of discovery before you become too creaky to climb on a plane, train or donkey. From this point onwards you must make every journey count.

David Dale – author, from *Essential Places*

I know how I am getting there. I just don't know where I am going to. I know where I am going to. I just don't know how I will get there.

Graham Taylor – managing director, Karakorum Expeditions, Mongolia

The Lower Zambezi National Park, a protected oasis. Mountains to the western side, the Zambezi snaking along the other. Wildlife abounds. It is 'wild' life – no people, just them. It is their land, we are only spectators.

Julie McIntosh – managing director of The Classic Safari Company

I recently read in the paper a story about drugs. The gentleman quoted in the article was referring to his experiences taking LSD. He said: 'For 40 bucks it is the cheapest trip you will ever have without leaving the country.' I recall the many thousands of dollars I have spent over the past ten years scaling peaks in South America, the Himalayas and Antarctica. This guy doesn't know what he has missed! No drug-induced experience can ever match the magic of seeing a pink dawn embracing an iceberg, and simply time to reflect while travelling to pristine natural environments.

Duncan Thomas – mountaineer and publisher

Travel is a necessary agony only to be endured
when there is an absolutely unchallengeable
reason to be somewhere else.

Ron Clarke – former Olympic athlete, chief executive officer
of Couran Cove Resort and author, from *Enjoying Life*

Climbing certainly shook me out of my middle-class complacency but did not divest me of my self-centred view of the world. Soon climbing took me to the Himalaya, where over half a dozen years I lost toes to frostbite, friends to avalanches, and almost died from rock-fall, ice-fall and exposure. Those were the bad times, but they were also the times which taught me about life and myself. A five-day descent from the summit of Annapurna II in a blizzard, not knowing whether we'd be alive at the end of each day, was an event which made me vow to live life to the fullest – this was not a licence for hedonism, but a decision not to waste opportunities and to find value in every experience.

Lincoln Hall – mountaineer, editor of *Outdoor Australia* magazine

When you travel, your mind can too. I've made so many little drawings on boarding passes that I'm sure one day I'll have an exhibition based on concepts from 40,000 feet. When all the world can travel, the world will be a better place.

Ken Done – artist

The reason why Conrad writes so well of the sea
is like any professional seaman, he fears it. People
who love the sea, who say they love the sea, are
the real amateurs. I never believe anybody when
they say that. I think: Well, you just don't know
much about it. It means they've been on a cruise
ship somewhere.

Anybody who's had to deal first-hand with the
sea and its real dangers knows its extraordinarily
mercurial nature – from being the friendliest
thing to the most dangerous – it's part of its
overwhelming fascination. Nothing could be
more tumultuous than the sea. It is a model of
chaos, of all the things that can go haywire.

Jonathan Raban – from an interview in the *New York Times*,
18 November 1999, author of *Passage to Juneau*

Writing about journeys, sometimes years after the event, is in effect travelling backwards. We should consider that travel accounts deliver not so much the facts – the supposedly *true* life – of a journey as a pastiche of partial recall, selective amnesia and dubious data. A travel story is not so much the true life of a journey as its unauthorised autobiography.

John Borthwick, PhD – travel writer, photographer and author, from *The Circumference of the Knowable World*

When I first started to travel overseas it was for commercial reasons, mostly urgent and short-lived. I would often enough wake up with a hangover in a hotel room that looked much the same as the last country I had been in, in a city in Asia hard to define from the last. I would do the day's business in a boardroom that could have been anywhere in the world and catch a plane to my next destination. As my job was mostly to trouble-shoot for a large multinational, I now refer to those times as my 'days of whine and neurosis'. Until one day I realised that I had travelled to twenty countries and had seen very little, and knew next to nothing about any of them. That was when I started to take two days off after business in every country I visited. Today, some thirty years later, I still have friends I cherish in a dozen countries.

A traveller's tip: Always visit the local markets, it's where the life of every country begins.

Bryce Courtenay, AM – author

Only when you have a good understanding of the different cultures, traditions and ways of life will you be considered a traveller rather than a tourist.

Mike Smith – travel editor for the *Daily Telegraph* and the *Sunday Telegraph*

You know, he paused and looked into the air,
Americans go half a world away looking for
something wonderful, and they don't realise it's
right there in Hawaii, or maybe in the Southwest.
It's a delusion to think you have to go far away
to see something special; but it's much more
difficult to understand what's special about a
place nearer home. I think you have to find a way
of seeing it, of changing the context so that what
is familiar appears in an unfamiliar way.
I would say that travel is all about that; finding a
way of seeing something and finding a way of
allowing a place to be revealed to you. Because
places have secret lives, you know. There's a
secret life of Hawaii, a secret life of San Francisco.
And the conventional traveller following
conventions doesn't see it.

Paul Theroux – author, from the *Houston Chronicle*,
2 July 1989

Above all, keep in mind the Traveller's First Commandment: 'Thou shalt not expect to find things as thou hast at home, for thou hast left home to find things different.' The most essential thing you can pack is an open mind.

Bill Peach – from *Holidays with Bill Peach*

Whenever possible, travel by train. It is by far the happiest and most humanising mode of travel, be it up the Khyber Pass or through Kyneton, Victoria, Australia and beyond.

The Hon Tim Fischer, MP

An oversized hand reached for mine and our eyes met; his peeping out over a large beak of a nose just like the falcons he would have seen on many journeys. We went into his small Chelsea flat and entered a world laden with memorabilia of Bedouin, camel dust, daggers and stories of exploration in the Empty Quarter of Arabia, and Kenya. I heard a personal account of Sir Wilfred Thesiger's remarkable life story, who for me is this century's greatest traveller. It is the people that make the place. My dreams of travelling are fuelled by rich memories of contacts with people who don't live in my other favourite place, 'home'.

Christine Gee – co-founder of Australian Himalayan Expeditions

Tourism can be a ritual in which by moving our bodies from here to there we summon up regenerative forces. It can provide the annual reward for a year's striving; some tourist journeys can be the event of a lifetime. We can gain prestige from tourism. We can 'find ourselves'. Alternatively, we can come back 'a different person'. Whether physically, intellectually, morally or spiritually, we can feel better after we have done some tourism.

Donald Horne – author, from *The Intelligent Tourist*

Before I took off for my first long trip overseas –
eight months backpacking around Asia – I sat on
Katoomba station late one night, waiting for the
Bathurst train, thinking: What must it be like to
wait for a train knowing that it doesn't really
matter when or where you arrive? Less than a
year later, sitting on another railway station,
watching a Thai sunrise, I experienced that
sensation of total freedom.
Twenty years later, its intoxicating sense is still
with me. To travel only knowing why, not where,
is one of the greatest experiences life can offer.

Andrew Denton – media personality

I came to the Himalayas to conquer Kopra Ridge,
but what I really conquered was myself.

Diane Armstrong – journalist and author, from *Mosaic:*
A Chronicle of Five Generations

After dinner, we lowered the zodiacs and were off again, chasing a fast-descending sun. The mountain light was so soft I felt as if I was experiencing a dream. All around me the hard-edged, high-contrast sandstone walls, icy seracs and crenellated, tessellated icebergs were enticed from stark daytime reality and led gently into the night. It was all done by the most enrapturing metamorphosis of light.

Howard Whelan – publisher *Australian Geographic*

I always create my most innovative software far
away from the computer on a lonely mountain.

Goronwy Price – president, Price Wizard Software

Travelling in a foreign country you are forced to depend on strangers in unfamiliar surroundings, to trust foreigners when one is lost or sick. At such times one needs some of a child's senses; the ability to express unconscious vulnerability and trust, a knowledge of the best people to approach for help, and of course the courage to ask a stranger. These are skills that adults often lack.

Denise Goodfellow – specialist guide, Northern Territory

When sailing a fleet of eleven square-riggers in the ghost lanes of the Roaring Forties in 1988 on the London-to-Sydney Australian Bicentennial First Fleet Re-enactment Expedition of Tall Ships, I flashed on the possibility of 'time travel'. You really know you are getting close to the truth when you feel the distinct presence of long-gone ancestors so strongly that you instinctively turn your shoulder, to see if they just might be there to welcome or guide you along the way.

Dr Jonathan King – historic re-enactment adventurer

I visited Malakula Island in Vanuatu because it was a primitive island with primitive customs. The men go around naked except for a banana leaf wrapped around their penis. That's primitive! Depending on what size belt they use to hold the banana leaf in place, determines whether they are a Big or Small Namba. There is no embarrassment in being a Small Namba, in fact they were such fierce warriors even the blackbirders kept away. I asked the natives how the island got its name.

Some French sailors landed there a couple of centuries ago. The natives wanted them to leave, so they offered copious amounts of kava and sat the sailors down on some stinging plants. When the Frenchmen sobered up, they ran around shouting: 'Mal a' cul, Mal a' cul', which meant 'pain in the arse', I believe. The name stuck.

Ben Cropp, AM – documentary maker, while filming *Legends of the South Pacific*

Trekking in the shadow of the Himalayas in Nepal always reminds me of the 'grass is greener' syndrome. Here the poor, bare-footed Nepalese, who have no roads and have to trek long distances for basic provisions, watch in bewilderment as they're passed by Western trekkers, who've left their high-rise city apartments and paid big bucks for the privilege of walking!

Greg Grainger – documentary producer and presenter

In earlier ages it was enough simply to travel.
However, these days just about the whole world
is accessible to everyone and your conscience
must be a factor in deciding where to go. The bad
news is that if you sit down with a world map
and look for a destination with complete social
justice, no discrimination and an economy and
culture that doesn't degrade the environment,
then you may as well resign yourself to forever
staying at home. But you can't do that either. If
the current trend to awareness continues, one day
Australian tourists may exert a positive influence
in the world and at home!

David McGonigal – travel writer

Innes's law of travel: The degree of lateness to catch the train/plane/bus is exponentially proportional to the likelihood of your partner's suitcase bursting open in the rush to the platform or check-in counter.

Stuart Innes – travel writer, life member and former president of the Australian Society of Travel Writers

A bed is a bed is a bed. The magic is outside.

Tony Sheldon – author, from *The Howl and the Pussycat*

Travel enhances the imagination. It is a longing
for the exotic that stimulates the soul.

W. Ted Wright, AM – chief executive officer of The
Commissary

On every road I travel, I *always* talk to strangers.

Jeff McMullen – reporter for *60 Minutes*

I am the eternal traveller, Badu – the dreamer, the fool. A travelling soul. Let me walk the plains of this earth, the valleys, the desolated deserts, the endless seas. I'll rest later.

Yossi Ghinsberg – speaker and author, from *Heart of the Amazon*

. . . there is something in the long, slow lift
of the ship, and her long, slow slide forwards
which makes my heart beat with joy. It is the
motion of freedom.

D.H. Lawrence – author, from *Odd Man Out*

Six days at sea and I smell like a bilge rat. Swilling grog to ward off scurvy has left me with a tongue fit for nothing but sanding teak.

Note from the passenger log of *The Coral Trekker*, 1990, Whitsundays

Dakar is a steam bath with a view.

The *New York Times*

All man's troubles stem from a single cause: his inability to sit quietly in a room.

Blaise Pascal

Travellers continue, in very large numbers, to make trips to exotic, non-Western lands, which seem to answer to some of the old stereotypes; that simpler society, where faith is pure, nature unspoiled, discontent (and its civilisation) unknown. But paradise is always being lost. One of the recurrent themes of modern travel narratives is the deprivations of the modern, the loss of the past: the report on a society's decline.

Susan Sontag – author, from *Modern Destinations*

There are lots of mysterious things about boats,
such as why one would get on one voluntarily.

P.J. O'Rourke – author

In order to travel the path, you must become the
path.

Gautama Buddha

This is a land where airplanes track icebergs the size of Cleveland and polar bears fly down out of the stars. It is a region, like the desert, rich with metaphor, with adumbration. In a simple bow from the waist before the nest of the horned lark, you are able to stake your life, again, in what you dream.

Barry Lopez – author, from *Arctic Dreams*

It wasn't a very lucky ship. The day before the
cook jumped overboard, an engine broke down
and we had to go at half-speed most of the day;
and then a woman in the first class fell asleep
with a lighted cigarette in her hand and set fire to
her bed and herself. It was very hot and then it
was very cold, as if we were living through the
seasons. Mexico went backwards at twenty knots
over the edge of the world.

Graham Greene – author, from *The Lawless Roads*

Hanoi is a city caught in the warp of time, a place of history and icons, some dead, some still living to remind one that here the past never dies.

Neil Sheehan – author, from *Two Cities: Hanoi and Saigon*

It is a truism that all cities are shaped by politics.
But it is true nevertheless – and true, to a
spectacular and insistent degree, of Barcelona.

Robert Hughes – author, from *Barcelona*

So, just as greater meaning could be read into the house with the eggshell lilac walls and the white-painted rattan chairs, so a greater understanding became possible of the long, patient line of dark men and women on one side of the road on the morning I had arrived: not just the poor of India, but an expression of the old internal cruelty of that poverty: people at the bottom, full of emotion, with no politics at that moment, just rejecting rejection.

V.S. Naipaul – author, from *India*

Change in Indonesia is rapid and sometimes depressing. Today's luxuriant forest is tomorrow's bare hillside, and today's mountain tomorrow's copper mine. I was at pains to avoid areas that had succumbed to tourist influences, for mass tourism is the great destroyer of customs and cultures, and the purveyor of uniformity.

Norman Lewis – author, from *An Empire of the East: Travels in Indonesia*

Wallace confounds the usual image of the Victorian explorer which is based largely on the African model. He did not go forward, rifle in one hand, Bible in the other, on the lookout for big game or souls to save. Nor did he seek to map the source of great rivers or to climb the peaks of the highest mountains.

Tim Severin – author, from *The Spice Islands Voyage: In Search of Wallace*

The ice fields are crossed forever by a man in chains. In the farther distance, perhaps, a herd of reindeer drifts, or a hunter makes a shadow on the snow. But that is all. Siberia: it fills one-twelfth of the landmass of the whole earth, yet this is all it leaves for certain in the mind. A bleak beauty, and an indelible fear.

Colin Thubron – author, from *In Siberia*

Kilimanjaro is a snow-covered mountain 19,710 feet high, and is said to be the highest mountain in Africa. Its western summit is called the Masai 'Ngaje Ngai', the House of God. Close to the western summit there is the dried and frozen carcass of a leopard. No-one has explained what the leopard was seeking at that altitude.

Ernest Hemingway – author, from *The Snows of Kilimanjaro*

Sir Edmund Hillary and Tenzing Norgay: 'The two of them rose above celebrity to stand up for the unluckier third of humanity who generally cannot spare the time or energy, let alone the money, to mess around in mountains.'

Jan Morris – travel writer, *Time Almanac 2000*

If there's anything I'm looking for in my travel, it's looking at the way people live and organise their lives and societies, the things they do to make life comfortable and pleasant. I'm lucky that I still have that curiosity. I thought I would lose it one day, but one thing I still love is setting off in the morning and just walking. I'm still as interested in seeing what's around the corner as ever. I love that feeling when you get to a junction and you think: Do I go left or do I go right? I love that.

Bill Bryson – travel writer, from an interview in the Good Weekend, *Sydney Morning Herald*, 20 February 1999

In May 1953, Edmund Hillary and Tenzing Norgay made the first successful ascent of Mt Everest, the world's highest mountain. From this climb developed a deep and enduring relationship between Sir Edmund and the people of the Solu Khumbu district, of the Everest region in Nepal. The first formal assistance from Sir Edmund was the Khumjung school built in response to a village elder's request to build a school. The Kunde and Paphlu hospitals, together with numerous village health clinics, have been built and continue to be staffed by the Himalayan Trust. Sir Edmund established the Trust to provide facilities for the villages of the Mt Everest region. No activity is undertaken without the suggestion, consultation and assistance of the local people.

If you would like to contribute to Sir Edmund Hillary's Himalayan Trust please send your donation to:

The Himalayan Trust
28a Remuera Road,
Auckland, New Zealand